HAL•LEONARD

INSTRUMENTAL
PLAY-ALONG

AUDIO
ACCESS
INCLUDED

PLAYBACK+
Speed • Pitch • Balance • Loop

TENOR SAX

Disney

Aladdin

T0079122

Audio arrangements by Peter Deneff

To access audio visit:
www.halleonard.com/mylibrary

Enter Code
6711-7034-4431-3464

Motion Picture Artwork TM & Copyright © 2019 Disney

ISBN 978-1-5400-6237-6

HAL•LEONARD®

Visit Hal Leonard Online at
www.halleonard.com

Contact us:
Hal Leonard
7777 West Bluemound Road
Milwaukee, WI 53213
Email: info@halleonard.com

In Europe, contact:
Hal Leonard Europe Limited
42 Wigmore Street
Marylebone, London, W1U 2RN
Email: info@halleonardeurope.com

In Australia, contact:
Hal Leonard Australia Pty. Ltd.
4 Lentara Court
Cheltenham, Victoria, 3192 Australia
Email: info@halleonard.com.au

Contents

ARABIAN NIGHTS
(2019)

TENOR SAX

Music by ALAN MENKEN
Lyrics by HOWARD ASHMAN,
BENJ PASEK and JUSTIN PAUL

ONE JUMP AHEAD

TENOR SAX

Music by ALAN MENKEN
Lyrics by TIM RICE

FRIEND LIKE ME

TENOR SAX

Music by ALAN MENKEN
Lyrics by HOWARD ASHMAN

To Coda ⊕

mf

f

D.C. al Coda
(with repeat)

CODA
⊕

ff

f

PRINCE ALI

TENOR SAX

Music by ALAN MENKEN
Lyrics by HOWARD ASHMAN

Slower, accelerating gradually

SPEECHLESS

TENOR SAX

Music by ALAN MENKEN
Lyrics by BENJ PASEK
and JUSTIN PAUL

Moderately
Piano

A WHOLE NEW WORLD

TENOR SAX

Music by ALAN MENKEN
Lyrics by TIM RICE